AF599202

SEL CAREERS

OCCUPATIONAL THERAPIST

BY STEPHANIE FINNE

BLUE OWL BOOKS

TIPS FOR CAREGIVERS

Social and emotional learning (SEL) helps children manage emotions, create and achieve goals, maintain relationships, learn how to feel empathy, and make good decisions. The SEL approach will help children establish positive habits in communication, cooperation, and decision-making. By incorporating SEL in early reading, children will be better equipped to build confidence and foster positive peer networks.

BEFORE READING

Talk to the reader about different types of therapy.

Discuss: There are therapists for different areas of health and well-being. Have you ever been to therapy? What kind?

AFTER READING

Talk to the reader about occupational therapists and empathy.

Discuss: How do occupational therapists help others? What traits do they need to have? What can you do to show empathy?

SEL GOAL

Some students may struggle with social awareness, making it hard to empathize with others. Help readers develop these skills by learning to stop and think about others. How can they help someone else? What do they need to do to empathize with another? How can they motivate themselves and others? Discuss how learning to do these things can help them build relationships.

TABLE OF CONTENTS

CHAPTER 1

WHAT IS AN OCCUPATIONAL THERAPIST?

Kenzi has a hard time holding a pencil and writing. She works on building these skills. How? She spends time with an occupational therapist.

Occupational therapy (OT) helps people practice daily tasks. This can include skills for school, like writing, or for home, like getting dressed.

Occupational therapists help people with **physical**, thinking, and **sensory** challenges. They help people of all ages. Some work with children in schools. Others work with people in clinics or hospitals. Some work with people in the community. This could be at a retirement home or a homeless shelter.

WHAT DOES IT TAKE?

Occupational therapists do not give up on their patients. They take time to listen to patients. They find out what is important to them.

Occupational therapists need a four-year college degree. They also need a **master's degree**. Then, they complete several months of training in different settings. During this time, they work with experienced therapists.

Therapists pass an exam to become **registered**. They take courses every three years to keep their registration. They also need a **license** for the state they work in.

CHAPTER 2

WHO DO THEY HELP?

Sometimes Theo feels like there is too much noise in his classroom. To help, he does OT at school. He works on what to do when he feels like there is too much noise.

OT can also help with **mental health** challenges. How? Therapists guide **mindfulness** exercises.

OT can help teach **social** and communication skills. It can help people deal with strong emotions like anger and sadness.

Damien and his occupational therapist act out situations. They work on meeting new friends. Damien practices what he can say and do.

OT helps people who have broken bones, burns, or other injuries. How? It helps them find new ways to do things.

Soshea has **cerebral palsy**. She goes to OT every week. She practices putting on her leg braces.

TYPES OF THERAPY

Physical therapy (PT) is another kind of therapy. PT helps with pain, strength, and movement. OT helps people practice important daily tasks.

leg brace

Zip

Jackson works on **fine motor skills**. He practices using scissors and lacing his shoes. He also works on **life skills**, like opening doors. This helps him get around on his own.

CHAPTER 3

HOW DO THEY HELP?

What happens when you go to OT? First, an occupational therapist does an **assessment**. They watch, listen, and learn about your needs. Then, they make a plan.

Therapists plan activities and games. They break them into simple parts. Why? These help patients practice skills.

Occupational therapists are **empathetic**. They help a lot of people. It is a career to be proud of!

WHEN DOES THERAPY END?

Occupational therapists help you set a goal. Then, they help you practice. They work with you until you meet your goal. It may take a long time or just a little while.

GOALS AND TOOLS

GROW WITH GOALS

To be an occupational therapist, you must be able to empathize with others. Try working on these goals.

Goal: Find one person to empathize with. Think about what their day is like. Think of what that would feel like.

Goal: Make a list of tasks that might be difficult for others. How can you help them with those tasks?

Goal: Occupational therapists are kind and caring. Practice for this career by being kind to someone today.

TRY THIS!

Think about the different things OT can help with. Research one of the conditions that a person going to OT might have. Learn more about the skills that might be difficult for them. What might they need help with? How could OT help them?

GLOSSARY

assessment
An evaluation of someone's abilities or needs.

cerebral palsy
A disability that shows as muscular incoordination and speech disturbances. It does not mean that a person has trouble with their thinking.

empathetic
Able to understand and share the emotions and experiences of another.

fine motor skills
Skills that involve the use of small muscles in the hands and arms. Examples are holding a pencil or turning a doorknob.

license
A permit or permission granted by a group to do something.

life skills
Skills that help you deal with life's challenges. This can be anything from tying shoes to dealing with emotions.

master's degree
A degree given by a college or university usually after one or two years of additional study following a bachelor's degree.

mental health
Health care that deals with the improvement of mental health.

mindfulness
A mentality achieved by focusing on the present moment and calmly recognizing and accepting your feelings, thoughts, and sensations.

physical
Relating to the body.

registered
Certified to do something.

sensory
Relating to the senses.

social
Relating to other people.

TO LEARN MORE

Finding more information is as easy as 1, 2, 3.

1. Go to www.factsurfer.com
2. Enter "**occupationaltherapist**" into the search box.
3. Choose your book to see a list of websites.

INDEX

Blue Owl Books are published by Jump!, 5357 Penn Avenue South, Minneapolis, MN 55419, www.jumplibrary.com

Library of Congress Cataloging-in-Publication Data

Names: Finne, Stephanie, author.
Title: Occupational therapist / by Stephanie Finne.
Description: Minneapolis, MN: Jump!, Inc., [2024]
Series: SEL careers | Includes index.
Audience: Ages 7–10
Identifiers: LCCN 2022061315 (print)
LCCN 2022061316 (ebook)
ISBN 9798885246347 (hardcover)
ISBN 9798885246354 (paperback)
ISBN 9798885246361 (ebook)
Subjects: LCSH: Occupational therapists—Juvenile literature. | Occupational therapy—Vocational guidance—Juvenile literature.
Classification: LCC RM735.4 .F56 2024 (print)
LCC RM735.4 (ebook)
DDC 615.8/515023—dc23/eng/20230125
LC record available at https://lccn.loc.gov/2022061315
LC ebook record available at https://lccn.loc.gov/2022061316

Editor: Eliza Leahy
Designer: Molly Ballanger
Content Consultant: Rachel Adler, MOT, OTR/L

Photo Credits: aquaArts studio/iStock, cover; Doro Guzenda/Shutterstock, 1; Auttapon Wongtakeaw/Shutterstock, 3; South_agency/iStock, 4; Igor Emmerich/Getty, 5; GBZero/Shutterstock, 6–7; fizkes/Shutterstock, 8–9; antoniodiaz/Shutterstock, 10; xavierarnau/iStock, 11; Andrey Sayfutdinov/iStock, 12–13; Maria Sbytova/Shutterstock, 14–15; FatCamera/iStock, 16–17, 20–21; Prostock-studio/Shutterstock, 18; Phynart Studio/iStock, 19.

Printed in the United States of America at Corporate Graphics in North Mankato, Minnesota.